I0818551

UNBREAKABLE SPORTS RECORDS?

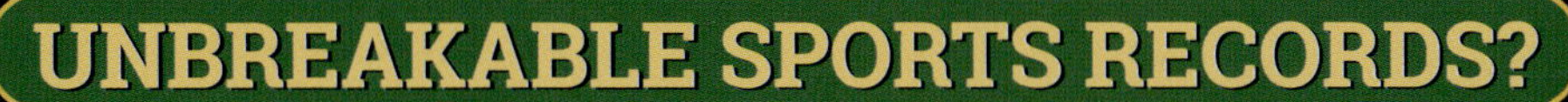

FOOTBALL RECORDS

THAT WILL BE TOUGH TO BEAT

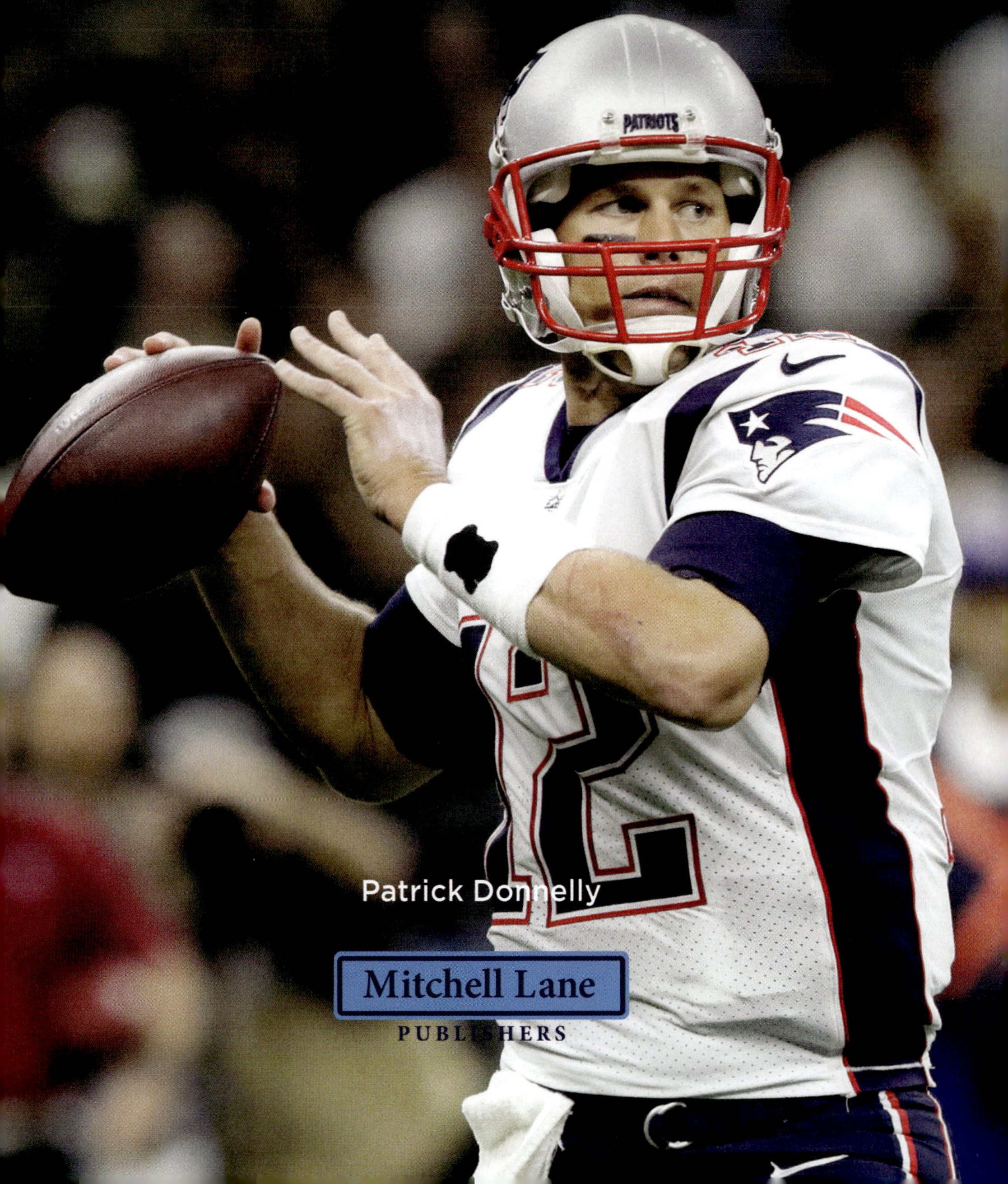

Patrick Donnelly

Mitchell Lane PUBLISHERS

Mitchell Lane
PUBLISHERS

mitchelllanepub.com

2001 SW 31st Avenue
Hallandale, FL 33009

First Edition, 2026.
Author: Patrick Donnelly
Designer: Ed Morgan
Editor: Tammy Gagne

Series: Unbreakable Sports Records?
Title: Football Records That Will Be Tough to Beat

Library bound ISBN: 979-8-89260-724-7
eBook ISBN: 979-8-89260-731-5

Photo credits: cover, p. 7, 8, 13, 15, 17, 19, 23, 25, 27, 29, 33, 35, 37, 39, 43, 45, 47, 51, 53, 55, 57 Alamy;
p. 4-5, 58 freepik.com

CONTENTS

INTRODUCTION

A GREAT START

Barry Sanders was a magician on the field. The former Detroit Lions running back could seemingly make himself disappear when a would-be tackler was closing in. Then he'd reappear down the field, trotting into the end zone for a touchdown.

One of his best runs came in a playoff game against the Dallas Cowboys in January 1992. Sanders took a handoff near midfield and rushed to his right. A crowd of five Cowboys defenders **converged** on him. But Sanders absorbed the first hit, kept his balance, and slipped through the crowd. Once in the clear, he faked out the last defender so badly that the other player fell over as Sanders left him in the dust. Sanders then ran the last 30 yards to the end zone untouched.

It was a great run, but it was also a typical run for Sanders, who spent his career tying opposing defenders into knots. He joined the Lions as a **rookie** in 1989. For the next ten seasons, he averaged almost 100 rushing yards per game. He led the National Football League (NFL) in rushing yards in four seasons, including when he rushed for 2,053 yards in 1997. That made him only the second running back in NFL history to rush for at least 2,000 yards in a season.

Sanders was on his way into the record books. With just a few more good seasons, he would have more career rushing yards than any other player in the history of the NFL. But he never got there. Sanders retired at age thirty, just over 3,000 yards away from the record. He said he'd lost his passion for the game. It didn't help that despite his greatness, the Lions won just one playoff game while he was in Detroit.

Barry Sanders had a chance to break the NFL's career rushing record, but he retired earlier than most people expected.

Sanders's retirement shows the grind that football players go through year in and year out. It's a physically and mentally draining game. The players who stick around long enough are remembered among the NFL's all-time greats. Some of them set records that seem to be untouchable—until someone breaks them, that is. These players set the bar high with their amazing achievements. Time will tell, however, whether their records are truly unbreakable.

Barry Sanders was elected into the Pro Football Hall of Fame in 2004.

CHAPTER ONE

Derrick Thomas's 7 SACKS IN ONE GAME

A quarterback sack can be a game-changing play. When the defense brings down the quarterback behind the **line of scrimmage**, it can snuff out a drive, stop a big comeback in its tracks, or even cause a turnover.

The NFL didn't begin tracking sacks as an official statistic until 1982. For this reason, some great individual pass-rushing performances have almost certainly been lost to history. But since 1982, the Kansas City Chiefs' Derrick Thomas is the only NFL player to register 7 sacks in one game.

Thomas won the NFL Defensive Rookie of the Year Award in 1989, when he finished the season with 10 sacks and started building his reputation as one of the league's most feared pass rushers. Opposing offensive linemen certainly learned that at times, Thomas was literally unstoppable.

"You could do it exactly right and even come to the sideline, after you've given up the sack, and say, 'Coach, I did everything right,'" former Chargers offensive tackle Harry Swayne told NFL Films. "And Coach would say, 'You're exactly right, you did. Good luck next time.' That's Derrick Thomas."

Derrick Thomas lines up to rush the quarterback in a game against the Chargers.

CHAPTER ONE

The Chiefs were hosting the Seattle Seahawks on November 11, 1990. Thomas, a powerful linebacker, entered the day with 8 sacks in as many games that season. Arrowhead Stadium hosted a pregame ceremony to recognize Veterans Day. This added to the day's importance for Thomas. His father, Air Force Captain Robert Thomas, was shot down over Vietnam in 1972. His body was never found. "Patriotic pride, my dad, the pain. It all had me pumped," Thomas said, according to Rick Plumlee of the *Seattle Times*.

For three quarters, Seahawks left tackle Andy Heck had the assignment to block Thomas one on one. Thomas sacked Seattle quarterback Dave Krieg three times in the first three quarters. The third sack forced a fumble that the Chiefs recovered in the end zone for their only touchdown of the day. After that, the Seahawks decided to double-team Thomas the rest of the way. He later said he relished that challenge.

DERRICK THOMAS'S 7 SACKS IN ONE GAME

Thomas set his legendary record on the Chiefs' home turf, Arrowhead Stadium.

Thomas tormented Krieg from every angle. He ran around blockers to hit Krieg from behind. He blew through double teams to chase Krieg around the field. He sacked Krieg four more times in the fourth quarter. On Thomas's record-setting seventh sack, Krieg stepped up in the **pocket**, looking for a receiver downfield. But before he could make the throw, Thomas slapped the ball out of his hands. Heck recovered the fumble, but Thomas had his record.

Seattle, however, would have the last laugh. On the game's final play, Krieg scrambled to avoid what would have been Thomas's eighth sack of the day. Then he fired a 25-yard touchdown pass to tie the score. The extra point kick gave Seattle a stunning 17-16 win.

Fred Dean (left) played in the NFL from 1975 to 1985.

Whose Record Did Thomas Beat?

San Francisco 49ers defensive end Fred Dean set the post-1982 NFL record with 6 sacks against the New Orleans Saints on November 13, 1983. That mark has been matched four times since, including once by Derrick Thomas himself in 1998, but only Thomas has reached seven sacks in a game.

Thomas's 7 sacks put him at 15 for the season. That was already a team record with seven games still to play. He went on to lead the NFL with a career-high 20 sacks and 6 forced fumbles in 1990. He played eleven seasons with Kansas City and averaged more than 11 sacks per season. Thomas was named to the Pro Bowl nine times and was inducted into the Pro Football Hall of Fame in 2009.

Aidan Hutchinson

Chasing Thomas's Record

Dominant pass rushers come in all shapes and sizes. But matching a record like Thomas's would require an athlete who is young enough to be quick yet strong enough to power through blocks. Detroit Lions defensive end Aidan Hutchinson fits that description. He already had a 4.5-sack game in 2024. Although he suffered a season-ending broken leg a few weeks later, he was still only twenty-five years old when the 2025 season began.

CHAPTER TWO

Emmitt Smith's 18,355 RUSHING YARDS

On October 27, 2002, the Dallas Cowboys hosted the Seattle Seahawks. The crowd at sold-out Texas Stadium was buzzing. The fans were hoping to witness history. Dallas running back Emmitt Smith entered the game needing 93 yards to break the NFL's all-time career rushing record.

Smith burst onto the NFL scene as a rookie with 937 rushing yards and 11 touchdowns for the Cowboys in 1990. He then topped 1,000 yards in the next eleven seasons, which itself is an NFL record. Smith was the league's top rusher for four seasons between 1991 and 1995. And he helped lead the Cowboys to three Super Bowl victories over that span.

By 2002, however, the Dallas **dynasty** had fizzled out. Most of Smith's key teammates had retired or moved on to other teams. The Cowboys had finished 5-11 in each of the previous two seasons, and they'd match that mark again in 2002.

There wasn't much riding on the outcome of that late-October game against Seattle. Still, all eyes were on Dallas that day to see if Smith could make history. One man, who happened to have his own suite at Texas Stadium, was certain Smith would end up atop the NFL's all-time rushing list.

Emmitt Smith was one of the NFL's most consistent performers during his years with the Dallas Cowboys.

CHAPTER TWO

"Emmitt Smith is the best setter of goals and keeping his eye on that and striving to attain it," Cowboys owner and general manager Jerry Jones told Todd Archer of ESPN. "He's the best I've ever been around—on and off the field. Owners, coaches, TV executives, you name it. He had a vision of wanting to be the rushing champion."

Smith got off to a great start against the Seahawks. He broke off runs of 11 and 14 yards on Dallas's first drive. He added two more 10-yard runs later in the first quarter to give him 55 rushing yards on just nine carries in the game's first fifteen minutes.

In the second quarter, Smith carried the ball just four times for zero total yards. But he got rolling again in the third quarter, posting 25 yards on five rushes during a long Dallas touchdown drive. That left him just 13 yards short of the record when the Cowboys took possession at their own 27-yard line with 10:10 to play in the game.

Emmitt Smith stretches before a game.

The Cowboys wasted no time getting Smith the ball. He opened the drive with a 3-yard run. Then on second down, Smith broke off an 11-yard run to give him 16,727 career rushing yards, breaking the all-time rushing record.

The record-setting carry was a classic Smith run, too. He was hit just beyond the line of scrimmage, but he refused to go down. He kept his feet churning and gained 8 yards after contact. It's a trait common among the best running backs, including longtime Chargers star LaDainian Tomlinson.

"Emmitt broke more tackles than anybody I saw," Tomlinson told Archer. "Emmitt never went down from the first contact. And he always seemed to get that extra 3 yards at the end of the run, like, 'Oh, he's going down—oh, no, he got 3 extra yards.' That happened with him so much. Also, he was able to [break tackles] even in his older days."

Walter Payton was one of the most dynamic running backs in NFL history.

Whose Record Did Smith Beat?

Walter Payton played for the Chicago Bears from 1975 to 1987. He rushed for more than 1,000 yards ten times between 1976 and 1986. Payton probably would have been the only rusher other than Smith to post eleven straight 1,000-yard seasons, but he played only nine games in the NFL's strike-shortened 1982 season.

Smith's **durability** played a big role in the record. Over his thirteen seasons with the Cowboys, he missed just five games due to injuries. And he gained an amazing 5,789 yards after turning thirty years old. This is an age when most running backs are coasting toward retirement.

After the 2002 season, Smith moved to Arizona, where he played his final two years with the Cardinals. He pushed his record to 18,355 yards—and set NFL career marks with 4,409 carries and 164 rushing touchdowns. Along the way, he set a standard for NFL running backs that few have been able to approach.

Derrick Henry spent eight years with the Tennessee Titans before joining the Baltimore Ravens in 2024.

Chasing Smith's Record

Most NFL experts list Smith's record as the one most likely to stand the test of time. Running backs don't get as many carries in the modern, passing-friendly NFL. And most don't remain effective well into their thirties, due to the wear and tear on their bodies. Derrick Henry might be the active player with the best chance. He finished the 2024 season with 1,921 rushing yards. That was his ninth NFL season, and he averaged almost 1,300 yards per season. Henry would need another 1,000 yards per season for seven more seasons to chase down Smith's mark, but he's proven to be incredibly durable and effective so far.

CHAPTER THREE

Brett Favre's 297 CONSECUTIVE STARTS

The Green Bay Packers were once among the top teams in the NFL. They won five league championships in the 1960s, including the first two Super Bowls. But they lost their footing soon thereafter. From 1968 to 1992, the Packers made the playoffs twice and won just one postseason game. Little did the Packers and their fans know that their luck was about to change when they traded for an out-of-shape, third-string quarterback before the 1992 season.

CHAPTER THREE

The Atlanta Falcons selected Brett Favre with their second-round pick in the 1991 NFL Draft. He'd shown a strong arm at the University of Southern Mississippi, but he suffered a serious hip injury in a car accident after his senior season. Concerned that the hip problems could linger, many teams passed on him. The Falcons took a chance, but it didn't turn out as they'd hoped. Favre spent much of his rookie season enjoying the Atlanta nightlife rather than studying his playbook. He gained weight and fell out of favor with the Falcons coaches.

But Favre still had one important believer. Ron Wolf was hired as the Packers general manager late in the 1991 season. He had scouted Favre in college and thought the quarterback had a great arm. Before the 1992 draft, he traded Green Bay's first-round pick to the Falcons for Favre.

Brett Favre scrambles for extra yardage against the Chicago Bears.

CHAPTER THREE

The Packers already had veteran quarterback Don Majkowski, and he began the 1992 season as the team's starter. But Majkowski injured his ankle in the third game of the season. Favre came off the bench and struggled as Green Bay fell behind the Cincinnati Bengals, 17-3. But with the Packers trailing by 6 points in the game's final minutes, Favre marched the team 92 yards, capping the drive with a 35-yard touchdown pass to Kitrick Taylor. The Packers won 24-23, and a legend was born.

Favre made his first start for the Packers the next week. He remained the team's starting quarterback every game for sixteen seasons. The ironman streak survived many close calls, even beyond the injuries quarterbacks typically sustain. For instance, Favre's father suffered a fatal heart attack on December 21, 2003. Nobody would have blamed Favre for sitting out the next night's game at Oakland. Instead, he decided to play to honor his father. And in the first half, he threw for 399 yards and 4 touchdowns as the Packers blew out the Raiders.

Brett Favre proved to be one of the most durable quarterbacks in NFL history.

Favre's streak survived other hardships as well, including his wife's breast cancer diagnosis and the severe damage to his property caused by Hurricane Katrina in 2005. Through it all, Favre kept marching on. He announced his retirement on March 4, 2008, after starting 253 **consecutive** regular-season games and 22 straight playoff games.

However, Favre was known to change his mind, and later that summer he came out of retirement to join the New York Jets. He started all sixteen games for the Jets before again retiring. But that summer, he changed his mind again and signed with the Minnesota Vikings in August 2009. He spent two years as the Vikings' starter before the streak ended on December 13, 2010, when the forty-one-year-old sat out a game against the New York Giants due to a sprained shoulder. That ended a streak of 297 consecutive starts, but it shattered the previous record by 26 games.

Jim Marshall was a constant presence on the Minnesota Vikings' defensive line for two decades.

Whose Record Did Favre Beat?

Minnesota Vikings defensive end Jim Marshall established the NFL record with 271 consecutive starts. He started the final game of the 1960 season for the Cleveland Browns. Then he joined the expansion Vikings and started every game for the team's first nineteen seasons.

"That's unheard of in any sport. Maybe baseball, but in football, that's unheard of," safety Hussain Abdullah, Favre's teammate in Minnesota, told the Associated Press. "The quarterbacks, sometimes they get blindsided. They take all kinds of shots. Serious durability, serious."

Once Favre retired for good, the **accolades** began pouring in from around the NFL and beyond. He even drew praise from Cal Ripken Jr., who had set Major League Baseball's record for consecutive games played at 2,632. "Brett has had an incredible career, and his consecutive games streak is remarkable," Ripken said in a statement released after Favre's streak ended. "As a football fan, I cannot fathom his accomplishment, and I appreciate his dedication to and passion for the game. He is a true gamer and has provided us all with a lot of wonderful memories."

Jake Matthews has been the anchor of the Atlanta Falcons' offensive line since 2014.

Chasing Favre's Record

Atlanta Falcons offensive lineman Jake Matthews finished the 2024 season with a 178-game starting streak. He'll be thirty-three at the start of the 2025 season. He would need to keep rolling for another seven seasons to break Favre's record. But it's not unheard of for an offensive lineman to play until he's forty, so Matthews has a shot if he stays healthy.

CHAPTER FOUR

Peyton Manning's 55 Passing Touchdowns IN ONE SEASON

The Indianapolis Colts made Peyton Manning the first overall pick of the 1998 NFL Draft. The University of Tennessee quarterback had a great football **pedigree**. His father, Archie, played a total thirteen seasons as a quarterback for the New Orleans Saints, Minnesota Vikings, and Houston Oilers. And his younger brother, Eli, would follow in their footsteps, playing sixteen seasons at quarterback for the New York Giants.

But of the three, only Peyton is often called the greatest quarterback in NFL history. He played thirteen seasons for the Colts, winning a Super Bowl and leading the NFL in passing yards twice along the way.

CHAPTER FOUR

If Manning's career had ended right there, he would've gone down as one of the all-time greats. And in fact, it did look like his career might end after the 2010 season. He sat out the entire 2011 season when it took four surgeries to repair a damaged disc in his neck. At thirty-five years old, Manning wondered if he was done.

But physical traits were never Manning's strong suit. He had a decent arm, but nothing like the cannons attached to the shoulders of John Elway or Brett Favre. Manning was a slow runner who thrived when he was able to stand in the pocket and pick apart opposing defenses. His intelligence and experience set him head and shoulders above his rivals.

Peyton Manning was the face of the Indianapolis Colts for 13 seasons.

"There has been no better weapon in the NFL in the past seventeen years than Peyton Manning's brain," CBS Sports' Pete Prisco wrote in 2016. "You can have the legs of the great runners, or the big arms of the power passers, or the ballerina moves of the great receivers, or the brute power of a tight end like [Rob Gronkowski]. Give me Manning's brain and I will play you every single Sunday."

Alex Marvez of Fox Sports asked former Colts tight end Marcus Pollard what made Manning such a great passer, especially in the game's biggest moments. "Confidence, preparation and overall smarts," Pollard replied. "The guy just has an ability to see something before it happens."

When Manning and the Colts agreed to part ways after 2011, Manning knew he could still be an effective NFL quarterback. But nobody could have predicted what he'd do when he signed with the Denver Broncos in 2012. Manning went on to start every game for the next three seasons. And his 2013 season was truly one for the record books.

Tom Brady fires a pass for the New England Patriots.

Whose Record Did Manning Beat?

The New England Patriots went 16-0 in the 2007 season, and quarterback Tom Brady was a big reason for their success. Brady threw 50 touchdown passes that year, breaking Manning's mark of 49 set three years earlier.

Perhaps he was sending a message with his opening night performance, when he threw a career-high 7 touchdown passes against the Baltimore Ravens. It was the start of something special, and something historic. Manning remained at a blazing pace the rest of the season. He had at least 4 touchdown passes in nine games that year. He was held to 1 touchdown pass in just one game and wasn't shut out by any opposing defenses.

Manning had 47 touchdown passes with two games remaining. He was a few short of tying the record of 50 when the Broncos played in Houston on December 22, 2013. Through three quarters, he'd thrown just one more touchdown pass. But in the fourth quarter, he connected twice with wide receiver Eric Decker to tie the record. He then wrote his name in the record books with his 51st touchdown pass, a 25-yard hookup with tight end Julius Thomas. Manning threw 4 more scoring strikes in the Broncos' final game, giving him 55 for the season. No quarterback has thrown more than 50 touchdown passes in any season since.

The Buffalo Bills' Josh Allen is one of the game's brightest stars.

Chasing Manning's Record

The NFL is blessed with many talented young quarterbacks. Buffalo's Josh Allen just might be the cream of the crop. He hasn't missed a start since his rookie season in 2018, and the Bills' wide-open offense could put him in line to challenge Manning's record at some point.

CHAPTER FIVE

Tom Brady's 7 Super Bowl WINS

Coming out of the University of Michigan, Tom Brady wasn't expected to become an NFL star. The New England Patriots selected him in the sixth round of the 2000 draft. Scouting reports had Brady pegged as a career backup. He was slow and looked somewhat awkward on the field. But he had **intangible** qualities that made him one of the most successful quarterbacks in NFL history.

"He's one of those guys who, as different generations came through the league, he was able to evolve as a person," former Patriots linebacker Jerrod Mayo told Albert Breer of *Sports Illustrated*. "He was able to connect with different people, different races, different age groups. And that's huge, especially at one of the most important positions in sports, a guy that can just stand above it all and relate to people and build **rapport** with different groups of people on a daily basis."

Tom Brady keeps his eyes downfield, looking for an open receiver.

CHAPTER FIVE

After playing in just one game as a rookie, Brady took over for injured starter Drew Bledsoe early in the 2001 season. Brady's stats weren't particularly impressive. In fifteen games, Brady threw 18 touchdown passes and 12 interceptions. He averaged just shy of 200 passing yards per game. But one number stood out from the rest: The Patriots won 11 of Brady's 14 starts.

Brady's legend really started to grow in the postseason. New England shocked the NFL with three straight victories to win their first championship. Brady led the game-tying and game-winning drives in the fourth quarter of their first-round win over the Oakland Raiders. And after the Patriots blew a late 14-point lead over the St. Louis Rams in the Super Bowl, Brady calmly marched them 53 yards in the final 90 seconds. This set up Adam Vinatieri's game-winning field goal on the game's last play.

Tom Brady calls out signals for the Patriots.

CHAPTER FIVE

Brady was just getting started. The Patriots won two more Super Bowls over the next three seasons. They got back to the Super Bowl twice in the next nine years but then lost both times. A thirty-seven-year old Brady led them to another championship in 2014. That was the start of another mini dynasty that saw the Patriots win three Super Bowls in five years.

When the Patriots finished that run, Brady was forty-one years old. But he still wasn't done. After one more season in New England, Brady left for Tampa Bay in 2020. And that year, he led the Buccaneers to three road victories in the playoffs before winning his seventh Super Bowl in a 31–9 defeat of the Kansas City Chiefs.

Charles Haley was part of the 49ers' dynasty in the 1980s.

Whose Record Did Brady Beat?

Before Brady's record-setting run, no player had had more than 5 Super Bowl wins. Between 1986 and 1996, defensive lineman Charles Haley won 2 Super Bowls with the San Francisco 49ers and 3 with the Dallas Cowboys. Many other players now have 4 Super Bowl wins. Most of them played for the 1970s Pittsburgh Steelers or the 1980s 49ers. The Steelers won 4 titles in six years, and the 49ers won 4 Super Bowls in nine seasons.

CHAPTER FIVE

Incredibly, Brady stuck around for two more seasons. He led the NFL in pass attempts and completions in both 2021 and 2022 before he finally retired at age forty-five. Some people wonder how a quarterback could play that long and remain so effective. Former NFL quarterback Trent Dilfer told Sam Farmer of the *Los Angeles Times* that Brady's strongest quality was his drive to overcome any obstacle in his way. "It's a defined passion and **perseverance** towards a long-term goal," Dilfer said. "I think it's his grit. A lot of people talk about it. Every football coach, including myself, tries to explain it, tries to get their team and coaches to buy into it. Tom Brady is walking grit. He sweats grit."

Whether Brady's record will stand the test of time remains to be seen. It will be tough for any player to rack up more championships. Like some other records, this one just might be unbreakable.

Patrick Mahomes

Chasing Brady's Record

For any player to challenge Brady's record, he'd have to be talented and healthy, and also play for a reliable winner. Kansas City quarterback Patrick Mahomes won his third Super Bowl ring in 2023 at age twenty-eight. That puts him on pace to match, or pass, Brady if Mahomes and the Chiefs remain among the NFL's top teams for another decade.

Think FAST!

Test your new knowledge of football by answering the following questions.

1. **What holiday was being celebrated on the day Derrick Thomas had seven sacks?**
   A. Christmas
   B. Halloween
   C. Labor Day
   D. Veterans Day

2. **Whose career rushing record did Emmitt Smith break?**
   A. Barry Sanders
   B. LaDainian Tomlinson
   C. Walter Payton
   D. Derrick Henry

3. **Who was Brett Favre playing for when he broke the NFL's consecutive game streak?**
   A. Vikings
   B. Packers
   C. Jets
   D. Falcons

4. **Why did Peyton Manning sit out the 2011 season?**
   A. A contract dispute
   B. A players' strike
   C. An injury
   D. Retirement

5. **Where did Tom Brady play college football?**
   A. University of Michigan
   B. University of Tennessee
   C. University of Southern Mississippi
   D. Harvard University

Answers: 1. D 2. C 3. A 4. C 5. A

Glossary

accolades
Expressions of praise or admiration

consecutive
Directly following another instance

converged
Came together to meet at a point

durability
The ability to withstand wear, pressure, or damage

dynasty
A team or other group with a long history of success

intangible
Unable to be seen or measured

line of scrimmage
The spot on the field where a play begins

pedigree
The background or history of a person or thing

perseverance
The ability to keep doing something even if it is hard

pocket
In football, the area behind the line of scrimmage where the quarterback stands

rapport
A close relationship based on communication and mutual understanding

rookie
A first-year player

Find Out More

IN PRINT

Donnelly, Patrick. *Basketball Records That Will Be Tough to Beat*. Mitchell Lane Publishers, 2026.

Hanlon, Luke. *Tom Brady*. Abdo Publishing, 2023.

Roland, James. *The Next Generation: NFL Star Quarterbacks*. ReferencePoint Press, 2025.

ON THE INTERNET

NFL, n.d.
www.nfl.com.

Pro Football Reference, n.d.
www.pro-football-reference.com.

Pro Football Hall of Fame, n.d.
www.profootballhof.com.

Index

About the Author

Patrick Donnelly is a sportswriter and author who lives in Minneapolis, Minnesota. He's written more than 100 books about sports, many of them about football. He has covered the Minnesota Vikings for the Associated Press and *Viking Update* magazine. And for the sake of Vikings fans, he hopes the team gets back to the Super Bowl soon.